D0430521

BASIC
PRINCIPLES
IN
PIANOFORTE
PLAYING

© Photo by G. P. Kesslere, B. P.

MR. LHEVINNE AT THE KEYBOARD

BASIC PRINCIPLES IN PIANOFORTE PLAYING

JOSEF LHEVINNE

With a new Foreword by
ROSINA LHEVINNE

DOVER PUBLICATIONS, INC., NEW YORK

Copyright ©1972 by Dover Publications, Inc.
All rights reserved under Pan American and International Copyright Conventions.

Published in Canada by General Publishing Company, Ltd., 30 Lesmill Road, Don Mills, Toronto, Ontario.
Published in the United Kingdom by Constable and Company, Ltd.

This Dover edition, first published in 1972, is a republication of the work originally published by the Theo. Presser Company, Philadelphia, in 1924. The text had previously been published as a series in *The Etude*. A new Foreword has been written specially for the present edition by Rosina Lhevinne.

International Standard Book Number: 0-486-22820-7
Library of Congress Catalog Card Number: 74-157433

Manufactured in the United States of America
Dover Publications, Inc.
180 Varick Street
New York, N.Y. 10014

CHAPTER I

THE MODERN PIANO

The possibilities of the piano have been a matter of continual development. The highly developed instrument of today is the descendant of many attempts at perfection. When Bartolomeo Cristofori, in the early years of the eighteenth century, sought to improve the keyboard instruments he was manufacturing, he found that it was necessary to start out upon an entirely new line of attack. The instruments of the time (clavicembali, harpsichords, etc.) were limited in expression because the wires were plucked with quills, much as a zither is played. By inventing an instrument in which the wires were struck with hammers, instead of being plucked, he made a distinct departure. He called it the Forte-Piano, because it could play both loud and soft. Later, doubtless for euphony, it became the pianoforte, and then the piano. But it could do far more than play loud or soft. It permitted the production of different classes of sound quality within its range. These are controlled by touch; and it is because of this that one of the basic problems of its use is the matter of touch, with which we shall have a great deal to do in this series. Rubinstein called the pedal "the soul of the piano." But the pedal can be used like a

1

soul in purgatory or like one in paradise. The finest pedaling in the world, however, is worthless unless the student is familiar with the basic principles of touch.

Before entering the discussion of the matter of touch or technic, however, let us consider first of all the most important thing, a good foundation in real musicianship. Certain things cannot be skipped in the early lessons without appearing to the enormous disadvantage of the student in later years. Possibly here is the greatest waste in music teaching, poor or careless instruction in the earlier years. The teacher of beginners is a person of great importance in all education, particularly in music. In Russia the teacher of the beginners is often a man or a woman of real distinction. The work is not looked upon as an ignoble one, worthy of only the failures or the inferior teacher. These teachers are well paid. Of course, in America you are developing many teachers of beginners who have had real professional training for this work; but in the past there must have been some ridiculously bad teachers of elementary work, judging from a few of the so-called advanced pupils whom I have been called upon to teach.

The folly of paying a teacher a considerable fee for instruction that should have been given at the very beginning, is too obvious to comment upon. Surely a practical people like the Americans will rectify this.

THINGS THAT CANNOT BE SKIPPED

A complete knowledge of notation should be drilled into the pupil at the first lesson. It is all very well to sugar coat the pill for the lively American child; but the musical doctor must see that there is no needed ingredient left out of the musical pill.

The pupil, for instance, must know all about notes. He must be able to identify instantly the time value of any given note, its name on, above or below the staff. When I first came to

FOREWORD TO THE DOVER EDITION

I wish to express my gratitude to Dover Publications for deciding to republish *Basic Principles in Pianoforte Playing* by Josef Lhevinne. In my opinion, this book will be of great value to musicians and students alike. As one who taught and performed with Mr. Lhevinne for forty-six years, I would like to use this short space to call attention to some of the more important points that impressed me while re-reading this book.

Anyone who starts to study the piano must realize at once that a knowledge of *music* is essential to his pianistic development. As students in Russia, we were taught from the earliest age to strive for a perfect technique, in other words, "a complete command of the instrument." But *technique was never a goal in itself; rather, it was only a means* to express the ideas of the composer. From the outset it was instilled in us that music is one of the arts that requires a middleman to present it to the public, and that the performer has the tremendous responsibility of remaining true to the composer's ideas. This basic principle dominated the whole of our musical lives, both as teachers and performers.

In the attempt to represent the musical wishes of the composer as clearly as possible, it is important to make use of all the available resources. The first, of course, is the printed page; we always emphasized the importance of consulting the best edition, which is usually the *Urtext,* or the least-edited one. Josef and I never paid attention to words added by the editors, but any original phrase by the composer that gave the character and mood of the work we considered very important. This applied not only to the first word (such as "Allegro") but also to those that followed (such as "con brio"). It is amazing how many students come to their lessons without being aware of the composer's written indications for the tempo and mood of the work.

To further acquaint the student with the composer's intentions, we always stressed the value of reading about the lives of the great masters and of trying to understand their thoughts at the time they wrote their compositions. Likewise, it is very useful for the student to read about the environment and the conditions in which the great composers lived. An understanding of the ornamentation in Mozart's music, for example, can be enhanced by understanding the rococo architecture of his time or even the stylized patterns of dress that he followed so carefully.

Once the student learns to understand and to respect the composer's ideas, then the various aspects of piano technique can be put to their proper use. Among the many practical and specific suggestions that Mr. Lhevinne puts forth in the following pages, it is difficult to single out any special ones for comment. But I do find it significant that quite a long chapter is devoted to "The Secret of a Beautiful Tone." Anyone who had the opportunity of hearing him play, or to a lesser degree of hearing his records, knows how incredible were his achievements in this area. It is unfortunate that he made so very few records.

Our years of teaching were a great source of pleasure for us both, and one reason for this was that we were both in some ways flexible. An example of this is in the area of phrasing. One of our principles was always to insist that the student find the long line of the melody and analyze at what point its peak occurs. (Josef always said that to have two peaks in the same phrase would be like having two heads on one torso.) We agreed that each phrase must have one high point—but as to where that point was, we often felt quite differently.

Once I taught one of his students while he was away on tour. When he returned, he gave the student a lesson. There was a phrase about which we evidently disagreed, and when the student played it "my" way, he asked: "What idiot taught you that?" The answer was: "Mrs. Lhevinne." But that was the exception that proved the rule. We did not always agree, but we generally respected the other's opinion.

Even now, in my own work with my two most capable assistants, I continue to teach in the same way, leaving them complete freedom to say whatever they think. As my husband so often said, "one of the great beauties of music is that it is not mathematics, where 'two and two' is 'four' and 'five' is wrong."

In closing, I would like to express my thanks to my esteemed colleague, Beveridge Webster, who last summer, when we both taught at Aspen, brought me the wonderful news that Dover (Mr. Webster's publisher) intended to reprint these condensed thoughts of Mr. Lhevinne. I am also very grateful to Mr. Hayward Cirker of Dover for suggesting that I write this foreword.

January 11, 1971

ROSINA LHEVINNE

CONTENTS

BASIC
PRINCIPLES
IN
PIANOFORTE
PLAYING

America, seventeen years ago, I gave some lessons. I find now that in the interim, there has been a great advance in methods of early instruction in America; but many students still indicate the most superficial early training.

Indifference To Rests

One indication of this is the indifference to rests. Rests are just as important as notes. Music is painted upon a canvas of silence. Mozart used to say, "Silence is the greatest effect in music." The student, however, does not realize the great artistic value of silence. The virtuoso whose existence depends upon moving great audiences by musical values knows that rests are of vital importance. Very often the effect of the rest is even greater than that of the notes. It serves to attract and to prepare the mind. Rests have powerful dramatic effect. Chaliapin has an instinctive appreciation of rests; and any one who has heard the great Russian's recitals knows that his rests are often as impressive as the tones of his gorgeous voice. Indeed, poise in music is often largely a matter of the correct observance of the full value of rests.

Sometimes it takes courage, seemingly, for the student to value a rest properly. He has the feeling that the audience is impatient and that he must go on playing. There must be sound. The composer, in creating the composition, did it with a distinct design in mind. That is the element of balance and symmetry which is natural to art. The student who plays a half rest with the value of a quarter rest destroys this artistic symmetry. The audience unconsciously feels this, and the work of the student does not please.

Examples I–1 and I–2 may be cited as examples of the dramatic value of rests. The first is from the *F Major Ballade* of Chopin. Hurry over this rest at the end of the composition and the value of a beautiful art work is destroyed.

No. I-1

Chopin Ballade, Op. 38

The second example is from the Chopin *Nocturne No. 13 in C Minor.* Here the rests are in the right hand. "But the left hand continues to play," you say. Of course, but nevertheless you must feel the rests. If you were singing this beautiful melody, or playing it upon the flute or the violin, you would have to feel the rests. I don't know what it is; but when you have that feeling in your mind you will bring it out in your playing, and your playing will be correspondingly more beautiful. There are thousands of passages of similar intent, in different pieces.

No. I-2

Chopin Nocturne, Op. 48, No. 1

One remedy is to imagine the melody as heard from an instrument of different quality from the piano—say the oboe, or the French horn. Another remedy is to play each hand alone, strictly observing the time and feeling the rests. This excerpt from Chopin makes a most excellent example; and the pupil who practices it religiously for a little while will gain a new respect for rests.

The reader is probably surprised by this time that I have taken up so much time with something that is not music at all, but silence. Well, it is upon such "little" things that all really important artistic progress must be based. Take the matter of note alterations. There are really three forms of staccato; but the average careless student either does not know about them or he plays all forms in the same identical manner.

The first form with the point

is the shortest. This might be represented as cutting off three-fourths of the value of the note and leaving only one-quarter, thus:

The second form is the dot:

which cuts the note in half, thus:

The third form is the dot and the dash,

which slices off only one-quarter of the note and leaves three-quarters to be played, thus:

This touch is sometimes called portamento; and it has a very distinct and important effect. These conceptions are general. They must not be taken too literally.

DEVELOPING RHYTHM

Before leaving these elements of musicianship, I feel it incumbent to point to the need for a fine development of rhythm. American students are capable of wonderful rhythmic development; but they have been limited in their opportunities. They hear jazz and ragtime from morning to night, and come to learn one rhythm and one rhythm only. They should be taught, early in life, all sorts of rhythmic designs. They should be taught that the rhythm must remain, although the moods may vary the rapidity of the tempo. They should be taught to develop a rhythmic sense like the Gypsies.

It is very hard to teach rhythm. It must be felt. It is contagious to a certain extent; and for that reason the student who attends concerts and who hears fine rhythms upon the various mechanical sound-reproducing machines has distinct advantages.

Duet playing, with a strong, vigorous musical individual, is one of the best ways in which to "catch" rhythm as one might catch the measles. Rhythm is infectious. A Strauss waltz under the baton of the Waltz King, or a Sousa march under the baton of the March King, never failed to sway thousands.

It is next to impossible to describe what rhythm is. It is by no means entirely a matter of accents. I have known pupils to play the Schubert *Marche Militaire* with every accent in the right place, and yet it sounded like a march of wooden soldiers, instead of live ones. It jerked and bobbed and banged and seemed to be devoid of the spring and snap that a good march should have.

The rhythmic design should, almost invariably, remain even though the movement itself changes in tempo. Some students preserve a rhythm all right at a certain tempo, but lose it entirely at a slower or a faster one. A good corrective is to ask them to think of the swinging pendulum. Fast or slow, the swing is identical, unless it is disturbed by some foreign body.

HEAR RHYTHMIC MUSIC

The reader must have patience if I seem to proceed slowly; but I can never leave the subject of rhythm without a full consideration of all the best ways of developing it. Nothing puts me in a worse mood than the student who does not play in rhythm; because rhythm is spirit in music, the most human thing in music. Some look upon it as a trifle. It is about as important a trifle in music as are the engines on an ocean liner. Because the Bohemians, the Hungarians, the Spanish, the Polish and the Russians seem to possess it instinctively is not so much a matter of heredity as that they have heard rhythmic music from babyhood. Therefore, the student should hear all the rhythmic music possible.

Another·good plan is to accompany older and more rhythmic singers and violinists. Above all things, do not imagine that playing in time and observing the accents methodically is all that there is to rhythm. A live rhythm may be observed with the time changing every few measures. The audience soon knows whether it is a living thing which the performer is creating, something with the pulse of the life-blood of music

running through it. Make your rhythms live and your playing
will live and be beautiful. Finally, you will be able to play two
rhythms at one time as in Examples I–3 and I–4.

No. I–3   Chopin Valse, Op. 42

No. I–4   Chopin Etude

In the next section of this series we shall discuss certain very
direct phases of the work of the student—not so much in their
bearing upon general musicianship as in their relation to the
keyboard.

CHAPTER II

GROUNDING IN MUSICIANSHIP

In our first discussion of this subject we dwelt at considerable length upon the fact that before the student even considers the matters of technic and touch, a good grounding in real musicianship is necessary. I cannot leave this phase of the matter without pointing out that a knowledge of the keys, the common chords, and the seventh chords, should be as familiar to the student as his own name. This would not be mentioned were it not for the fact that I have repeatedly had students come for instruction who have after great effort prepared one, two, or at the most three show pieces, even pieces as far advanced as the Tchaikowsky or the Liszt Concerto, who barely knew what key they were playing in. As for understanding the modulations and their bearing upon the interpretations of such complicated and difficult master works, they have been blissfully ignorant.

Study of this kind is not only a great waste of the pupil's time but also a disgusting waste of the time of the advanced teacher, who realizes that he is not training a real musician but a kind of musical parrot whose playing must always be meaningless. Often these pupils have real talent and cannot be

9

blamed. They simply have had no teacher in the early years with patience and sufficient will power to hold them back until they have been exhaustively drilled in scales and arpeggios. A smattering will not do. They must know all the scales in all the keys, major and minor, and they must literally "know them backwards." They must know the inter-relationship of the scales; for instance, why G♯ minor bears a harmonic relationship to C♭ major.

The scales should be known so well that the student's fingers will fly to the right fingering of any part of any scale instinctively. The trouble with many students is that they attempt difficult problems in what might be termed musical calculus or musical trigonometry without even ever mastering the multiplication table. Scales are musical multiplication tables. One good way of fixing them in the mind is to start to play the scales upon the different tones of the key consecutively.

Take the scale of E major, for instance. Play it first this way, starting with the keynote:

Ex. II-1

Next start with the second note of the scale with the second finger, thus:

Ex. II-2

Then with the third finger, thus:

Ex. II-3

Then with the fourth note with the thumb, thus:

Ex. II-4

Continue throughout the whole scale; and then play them in similar manner with the right and the left hand together. Treat all the scales in the same manner.

Most pupils look upon scales as a kind of musical gymnasium for developing the muscles. They do that, of course, and there are few technical exercises that are as good; but their great practical value is for training the hand in fingering so that the best fingering in any key becomes automatic. In this way they save an enormous amount of time in later years. They also greatly facilitate sight reading, because the hand seems to lean instinctively to the most logical fingering, to elect it without thinking. Take it for granted, you may have too little scale practice, but you can never have too much.

The study of harmony is also a great time saver in piano playing. Know the chords and know the fingering of all the arpeggios, which is really logical fingering of most of the common chords. Don't pay a teacher a high fee later in your musical life to have him point out something that you should have learned in the musical primary class.

THE VALUE OF EAR TRAINING

Ear training is also of very great importance. Most students hear, but they do not listen. The finest students are those who have learned how to listen. This becomes an axiom with teachers of advanced pupils. The sense of aural harmony cannot be too definitely developed. The pupil who cannot identify chords, such as the common chords, and the seventh chords, by ear, stands about as much chance of entering the higher realms of music as the student who does not understand a word of Latin does of comprehending a page from Virgil when he hears it read to him.

There is no way of dodging or sidestepping this knowledge. I am obliged to say a hundred times a week, "Listen to what you are playing."

Absolute pitch is by no means absolutely necessary. I have it and have always had it. Safonoff, my own master, did not. Rubinstein did. Sometimes it is a disadvantage. I cannot think of any composition except in the key in which it was written. Sometimes when a piano is a whole tone flat or a half tone sharp, I become fearfully confused, as it does not seem that I am playing the right notes. I instinctively start to transpose the sounds to where they belong and thus get mixed up.

Essentials of a Good Touch

The matter of touch is so all-important that the remainder of this section will be devoted to the subject. Even then, we cannot hope to cover more than a fraction of the things that might be said. Have not whole books been written upon the subject? Indeed, there is now in the different languages of the musical world, what might be called a literature of touch.

First of all, let us consider our playing members, the fingers, the hand, with its hinge at the wrist to the arm, and finally the torso—all of which enter into the problem of touch. With me, touch is a matter of elimination of non-essentials, so that the greatest artistic ends may be achieved with the simplest means. This is a general principle that runs through all the arts. Thus, in the manipulation of the fingers on the keys, I direct my pupils to cut out any action upon the part of the fingers except at the metacarpal joints.

The metacarpal joints are the ones that connect the fingers to the hands. Of course, there are exceptions, when the other joints of the fingers come into play. These we shall discuss later; but for the main part we shall progress far more rapidly if we will learn the great general principle of moving the fingers only at the joint where the finger is connected with the body of the hand. There was a time, I am told, when the great aim of the piano teacher was to insist that the hand be held as stiff and hard as a rock while the fingers rose to the position shown in Figure 1, in which all of the smaller joints were bent or crooked, and then the finger descended upon the key like a little sledgehammer. The effect was about as musical as though the pianist were pounding upon cobblestones. There was no elasticity, no richness of tone, nothing to contribute to the beauty of tone color of which the fine modern piano is so susceptible. Now, the finger arises in the position shown in Figure 2, and the movement up and down is solely at the point marked.

Fig. 1.

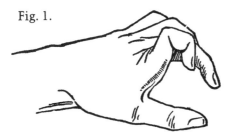

Fig. 2.

Movement at this joint only

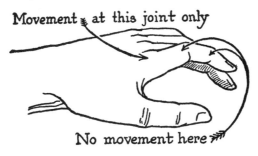

No movement here

Before proceeding further we have to admit that touch is largely an individual matter and that the nature of the player's hand has a great deal more to do with it than most people imagine. In days gone by there was an impression that a long, bony, fleshless hand, with hard fingertips, was a good pianistic hand. It may be for execution of florid passages and great velocity; but for the production of a good tone it can be extremely bad.

Rubinstein had a fat, pudgy hand, with fingers so broad at the fingertips that he often had difficulty in not striking two notes at one time. Indeed, as I have pointed out hitherto, many of the so-called mistakes that he made were due to this condition. On the other hand, his glorious tone was in no small measure due to this. Indeed, it may be said that the thicker the cushions of flesh upon the fingertips, the wider the range of variety of touch. Rubinstein, by means of an unearthly amount of work at the keyboard, was able to overcome technical obstacles and get the benefit of the responsive cushions he had at the ends of his fingers. This is merely a mechanical and acoustical principle. It is easy to distinguish when one listens to a metal xylophone. If the bars of the xylophone are struck with a hard metal rod, the tone is harsh and "metallic." Let them be struck with a rod with the end covered with soft felt and the tone is entirely different and beautifully musical. You may not think this applies to the tone of the pianoforte; but a little experimenting will soon show that it is the case.

Amateurs with Naturally Fine Touch

It thus happens that many amateurs, who know little about music itself, possess a touch which is very beautiful merely because they have accidentally learned how to play with right arm conditions and with the proper part of their fingertips; so that, instead of delivering a bony blow to the ivory surface, they touch the keys with felt-like cushions of human flesh and produce a really lovely tone without knowing how they do it. With proper instruction along these lines, I shall hope to make clear in ensuing sections of this series that it is possible for the person with an inferior touch to develop his tone amazingly.

Of course, a brittle touch is quite as necessary at times as the mellifluous singing tone. Brilliancy is as important as "bel canto" in piano playing. One general principle, however, is that of striking "key bottom." Many students do not learn this. The piano key must go all the way down in the production of a good tone. The habit of striking it half way accounts for much white or colorless playing. Many students do this without knowing it. It is a habit that quickly grows upon one. More than this, it contributes a kind of hesitancy and lack of sureness to playing that is decidedly inartistic. The player never seems sure of himself.

During your next few practice periods, analyze your own playing and note carefully whether you are skimming over the surface of the keys. Unless you have had a very thorough early training, you will probably discover that one note in every ten is slighted. It may be just enough to give your whole playing an amateurish complexion. If you find that this is the case, return to the practice of slow scales and then slow, simple pieces with good melodies and simple chords. Scores of students play chords with some of the notes striking key bottom and others only half way down. The full effect of the harmony is thus lost. Of course, you may not suspect that you do this; but do you really know?

In the next section of this article we shall continue this discussion of beautiful tone-color, revealing what seems to be the real secret of a lovely singing tone. It is really quite a simple matter when the underlying principle is correctly understood. Of course, if the student has the privilege of studying it under a good teacher, it may be more rapidly acquired; but there is no reason why the main essentials cannot be told in print.

CHAPTER III

The Secret of a Beautiful Tone

It will be remembered that in the previous chapter of this series a promise was made that we would next attempt to determine the "secret" of a beautiful tone. In this connection it must be recollected that considerable attention was given to the matter of individuality. In the first place, every piano student who aspires to acquire a beautiful tone must have a mental concept of what a beautiful tone is. Some people are born with a sense of the beautiful in sound. They do not need to be told. It is like the finely balanced sense of color possessed by some, in contrast to those who are color blind. If you have this sense of tonal beauty you are lucky. If you do not have it, do not despair, because by hard work and experience in listening to pianists who do possess a beautiful tone, you may develop it. I have known innumerable students with a very disagreeable tone who have in time developed an attractive one by persistent efforts. However, if you are tonally deaf to lovely sound qualities there is very little hope for you.

On the other hand, there are those who have a natural tonal sense but who do not have the technical qualifications for producing good tone at the piano, and it is to those that my remarks are now directed. The adjustment of the hand and arm to conditions that produce good tone is half of the battle. That is, the student must get clearly in mind what contributes to good tone production on the keyboard. In work with my masters, in personal investigations of technical principles, and through hearing intimately most of the great pianists, from Rubinstein to the present, certain basic facts seem to be associated with those who have good tone in contrast to those who do not.

In the previous section we have spoken of the part of the finger that comes in contact with the keys. If that part is well covered with cushions of flesh, the tone is likely to be far better than if it were hard and bony. Therefore, the main principle at the first is to see that the key is touched with as resilient a portion of the finger as possible, if a lovely, ringing, singing tone is desired instead of the hard, metallic one. What part of the fingertip is this? Certainly not the part immediately behind the fingernail. There the tone produced is still bony and unresponsive. Just a little farther back in the first joint of the finger you will notice that the cushion of flesh is apparently more elastic, less resisting, more springy. Strike the key with this portion of the finger, not on the fingertips as some of the older European methods suggested. To accomplish this, I would call your attention to the illustration in Chapter II, in which it is distinctly stated that the finger moves as a whole and at one joint only—the joint connecting the finger with the body of the hand. If the fingers descend upon the keys in this fashion you will notice that they do not strike on but just a little behind the tips. In other words, the key is touched with as large a surface on the first joint of the finger as is feasible.

The Ringing, Singing Tone

It is almost an axiom to say that the smaller the surface of the first joint of the finger touching the key, the harder and blunter the tone; the larger the surface, the more ringing and singing the tone. Naturally if you find a passage requiring a very brilliant, brittle tone you employ a small striking surface, using only the tips of the fingers. This is just one of the elements of good piano tone; but it should be mastered by all progressive piano students. Indeed, this in itself will improve your tone immensely, even though you may not employ some of the other principles which we shall discuss later. Before dismissing the subject, let the student think for a moment of the luscious quality of tone which often accompanies melodic passages in which the thumb is used a great deal. This is due in no small measure to the large, springy cushion of flesh on the thumb, in contrast with the much smaller cushion employed with the fingers by the student who has been trained to strike with the very tip of the finger.

The Part the Wrist Plays in a Good Tone

Very few students realize the part the wrist plays in the production of a good tone. If they were compelled to ride at a high rate of speed over a rough road in an automobile without springs or shock absorbers, they would go through a very terrible experience. They would be jarred and bumped almost to death. Yet that is what many students actually do in their piano playing. If the cushions of flesh on the ends of the fingers are the pneumatic tires in piano playing, the wrist is the spring or the shock absorber. For this reason it is next to impossible to produce a good singing tone with a stiff wrist. The wrist must always be flexible. The more spring the less bump; and it is bumps that make for bad tone on the piano.

Of course, if you are playing a passage like that in Example III–1 from the Liszt *Campanella,* where the greatest possible brilliancy is demanded, a stiff wrist and pointed fingers are not only permissible, but absolutely necessary.

Ex. III-1   La Campanella - Liszt

Or a passage like that in Example III–2 from the Schumann *Papillons*, which should be an imitation of brass instruments, must be played with pointed fingers and stiff wrists.

Ex. III-2   Schumann Papillons, Op. 2, No. 12

The same is true of the lovely passage in Example III–3 from Moszkowski's *Etude in Double Notes, Opus 64,* only with a lighter touch.

Ex. III-3   Moszkowski, Op. 64, No. 1

The cultivation of a singing touch should be a part of the daily work of every student who has passed the first few grades of elementary study, if indeed it may not be introduced earlier with students of more mature intelligence. All sorts of exercises will be devised by the skillful teacher. One of the simplest is to take the simple scale as in Example III–4.

Ex. III - 4

Poise the hand about two inches above the keys. Hold the hand in normal position as you would upon the piano keyboard (not with the fingers drooping down toward the keys). Now let the hand fall a little with the first joint of the second finger, the wrist still held very flexible so that the weight of the descending hand and arm carries the key down to key bottom, quite without any sensation of a blow. It is the blow or the bump which is ruinous to good tone. The piano is not a typewriter to be thumped upon so that a sharp, clear type impression will be made. Rather imagine that you are actually playing upon the wires, ringing them with soft felt-covered hammers and not with hard metal bars.

As the hand descends for this swinging touch, the finger is curved normally; it is not held straight. As the finger touches the key-surface, it feels as though it were grasping the key, not striking or hitting it. There is a vast difference of sensation here. Always feel as though you had hold of the key, not that you are merely delivering a blow to it. Do not think of the ivory surface of the keyboard as you would of a table. That idea is entirely wrong. Those who play the piano as though they were strumming on a table will never get the innate principle of a good tone.

Again when the hand descends, as large a surface of the fingertip as feasible engages the key; and the wrist is so loose that it normally sinks below the level of the keyboard. Observe your hand sensations very carefully. The tone is produced in the downward swing of the hand. If it were possible to take one of the exaggeratedly slow moving pictures of this touch, there would be no spot, no place, no moment where the movement seemed to stop on the way down. If there were such a place it would produce a bump. The tone seems to ring out beautiful and clear. The key is touched "on the wing," as it were, in the downward passage. All this concerns only the first note of the melody or phrase. The other notes, if the melody is to be played legato, must be taken with the fingers quite near the keys, raising or dropping the wrist according to the design of the melody.

The student who values a good tone will have the patience to practice all his scales, in both hands, one finger at a time, until this principle becomes automatic, until it is just as natural as free and easy walking. He will find that his playing becomes more graceful, more pleasurable, more satisfying to his sense of tonal beauty and to his hearers. But he has to listen!

When he attempts a powerful forte passage later in his musical life, he will discover that he can make the piano ring with the greatest possible volume, without making it sound "bangy." The reason why a number of people say that they do not care for piano playing is that so many so-called performers upon the instrument treat it as though it were an anvil and go on hammering out musical horseshoes.

In Chapter I of this series some of the *Etude* readers may have been a little out of patience with the extent of my remarks about rests. If rests are important, the method of stopping the sound of the note is quite as important as the method of sounding it. The most superficial examination of the inside of the keyboard reveals that the sound is stopped by the felt damper coming against the strings. In brilliant compositions, such as, for instance, the Mendelssohn *Scherzo in E Minor,* in a passage like that in Example III–5, the sound may stop quickly and abruptly as in all full staccato passages.

Ex. III-5

But in melodic passages it is very offensive to have a "sound bump" at the end of the tone. Therefore, at the end of the tones in melodic passages the student reverses the process by which he produces the tone. The wrist must be gradually raised until the finger leaves the key, as an airplane leaves the ground; and, of course, the key itself ascends gradually and the damper touches the wire without the "bumping off" sound. Many, many students strike the keys right but do not seem to have mastered the very simple, but very vital principle of releasing them so that there is no jerkiness. Details? Aha—these are the details upon which those who aspire to be masters work their hardest.

Although we have reached the third chapter of our discussion of this fascinating subject—which has so much to do in determining how to play the instrument so that it will be really musical in contrast to the street piano—we have been able as yet to cover only a few of the main points. In the next chapter we shall take up the matter of how to acquire great delicacy of touch and its antithesis, great power. This will be illustrated by a rare Russian portrait of Anton Rubinstein in a position at the instrument in which we shall attempt to show how that famous "lion of the keyboard" produced some of his powerful effects.

CHAPTER IV

ACQUIRING DELICACY AND POWER

In the last chapter of this series the all important matter of securing a fine tone was considered. In this the reader will remember that, in addition to the ability to conceive a beautiful tone mentally, attention was called to the fact that richness and singing quality of the tone depend very largely (1) upon the amount of key surface covered with the well-cushioned part of the finger and (2) upon the natural "spring" which accompanies the loose wrist. While the following remarks may be read independently of the foregoing chapters, the student will do well to re-read them to fix certain fundamental principles in the mind.

In the matter of delicacy the student may well give earnest attention to anything which will contribute this exquisite quality to his playing when the composition demands it. To be able to play with the delicious lightness and beauty of Cluny lace should be the ambition of all students. A beautiful lace shawl is the best comparison I know to what I mean by delicacy in playing. There is lightness, fineness, regularity of design, but without weakness or uncertainty.

THE TECHNICAL SIDE

The technical side of the problem is not so difficult to explain. In the first place the upper arm and the forearm must feel so light that the player has the impression that they are floating in the air. The mental attitude here is very important. Delicacy is inconceivable with a heavy arm. The least suggestion of tightening or cramping of the muscles is literally fatal to delicacy. One may say "relax" the arm; but if the arm is completely relaxed it will do nothing but flop limply at the side. On the other hand, it can be held in position over the keys with entire absence of nervous tension or stiffening, with the "floating in the air" feeling that makes for the first principle of delicacy.

Before proceeding further it might be well to note that the player can actually think moods and conditions into his arm and fingers. His mental attitude means a great deal in the quality of his playing. Just as the voice immediately reflects in its quality the emotions of great joy, pain, sorrow, scorn, meanness and horror, so do the fingers and the arm in somewhat similar fashion respond to these emotions and represent them in playing for those who have mastered the technic of playing so that they are not concerned with details which should become automatic. Anyone who heard Rubinstein play will realize how the emotions can be conveyed to the keyboard in an altogether marvelous manner. No audience is immune to this appeal. The non-musical auditors, in fact, come more for this sensation than for any understanding of pure music. They know instantly when it is present and go away gratified and rewarded. They do not understand the musical niceties; but they do comprehend the communication of human sensations and emotions when sincerely portrayed by the pianist who feels that he has something more to do in his art than merely to play the notes.

FLOATING IN THE AIR

To return to the matter of delicacy. If the student has mastered the principle of the "arm floating in air" (and it is something to be gained more by the right mental attitude than by any specific practice), the next step is to realize that delicacy does not consist merely of lightness. There are thousands of students who can play with some degree of lightness but who miss or slight so many notes in the course of a composition that their playing is really irritating, even to the non-musical listener. Delicacy must not be secured at the sacrifice of completeness. For this reason, even in the most delicate passages, every key struck, black or white, must go all the way down to key bottom. This is most important. Don't have your lovely lace shawl filled with holes or worn places.

The third principle in the practical matter of securing delicacy is to play with the fingers on the surface of the keys. That is, when you raise your fingers you do not take them perceptibly away from the surfaces. This simple matter insures the player against too forceful a stroke and makes the playing more uniform. It is difficult to do, especially with impatient students; but the matter of delicacy should be studied at a slow tempo so that the student can analyze his finger and arm conditions. He should repeatedly interrogate himself:

IMPORTANT QUESTIONS

"Is my arm floating?"
"Am I striking each note to *key bottom?*"
"Am I keeping my fingers on the surface of the keys?"
In playing for delicacy the key is struck with the fingertip rather than with the fleshy ball as when producing the full round singing tone. I also notice that when I am trying to secure a "floating arm" condition, my elbow extends very slightly from the side of my body.

Practice for delicacy may be accomplished through thousands of pieces and exercises. The passages IV–1 through IV–4 are examples of particularly good material for use in this connection.

Ex. IV-1 Chopin, Berceuse

Ex. IV-2 Raff's La Fileuse

Ex. IV-3 Grieg, Butterfly

Ex. IV-4   Marche a la Turque, Beethoven-Rubinstein

POWER IN PLAYING AND WHAT IT MEANS

Every teacher encounters pupils who are physically very strong and who can easily produce noise at the keyboard. On the other hand there are pupils who are not particularly strong, but who play with very great power. What is the reason? Of course strength, real physical strength, is required to play many of the great masterpieces demanding a powerful tone; but there is a way of administering this strength to the piano so that the player economizes his force. I know of one famous pianist who has always inclined to the immovable torso or body in playing. He sits like a rock on the piano chair, producing all his effects by means of strokes or blows to the keyboard. Much of the great playing I have heard has been produced by altogether different means. Consider, for instance, the picture of Rubinstein presented herewith. The artist has caught something here which the photographer has missed in most of the portraits of Rubinstein at the keyboard. This was probably because Rubinstein may have posed when he knew he was before the camera. But this sketch is Rubinstein as I knew him. Notice that instead of sitting bolt upright, as the pictures in most instruction books would have the pupils do, he is inclined decidedly toward the keyboard. In all his forte passages he employed the weight of his body and shoulders.

HOW ANTON RUBINSTEIN SAT AT THE PIANO
From a Drawing from Life

This was most noticeable; and the student should remember that when playing a concerto, Rubinstein could be heard over the entire orchestra playing fortissimo. The piano seemed to peal out gloriously as the king of the entire orchestra; but there was never any suggestion of noise, no disagreeable pounding.

NATURAL SHOCK ABSORBERS

Why no noise? Because Rubinstein's wrists were always free from stiffness in such passages and he took advantage of the natural shock absorber at the wrist which we all possess. He employed in principle the touch we have discussed in previous chapters of this series and his playing assumed a power and a grandeur I have never heard since his time, but to which I always aspire as my life ideal in my public performances. He did not pound down upon the keyboard, but communicated his natural arm and shoulder weight to it.

There is a vast difference between the ordinary amateur hammering on the keyboard for force and the more artistic means of drawing the tone from the piano by weight or pressure properly controlled or administered. Take the first movement of the Chopin *Military Polonaise*, for instance (Example IV–5).

Ex. IV-5   Military Polonaise
Allegro con brio M.M. ♩=96

Play this first with stiff wrists and forearms, and notice how bangy and disagreeable it sounds. Now play it with the wrists loose, employing the fleshy parts of the fingers and feeling that the weight and power are communicated to the keyboard from the shoulder. This beautiful composition is often ruined by banging, whereas it may be delivered with a lovely tone and rich singing quality. The same is true of the *B-flat Minor Scherzo,* which is another of the musical anvils of the typical conservatory. If Chopin could hear how this is murdered, he would turn in his grave. Instead of being given with nobility and grandeur, its opening passages are banged out with sledgehammer blows that are altogether unforgivable.

There is an acoustical principle involved in striking the keys. If the blow is a sudden, hard, brutal one, the vibrations of the wires seem to be far less pervading than when the hammers are operated so that the wires are "rung" as a bell.

Accuracy in Playing

Because in his later years Rubinstein was now and then inclined to miss a note or so in the course of a recital, indulgent students have assumed that since the message of the master composer is so much more important than the little matters of technical details, they can improve upon Rubinstein and leave out a great many more notes. Rubinstein's playing in his youth was doubtless immaculate from the standpoint of accuracy. In his last years the bigness of his musical conceptions and the greatness of his soul were such that he burst all bonds to give his great message to the public. We can forgive Rubinstein anything; but in these days of keenest competition the student must look upon inaccuracies as unpardonable. The subject of accuracy is so important that we shall require more space for its discussion and it will be taken up in the next chapter along with The Basis of Fine Staccato.

CHAPTER V

ACCURACY IN PLAYING

Why is much playing inaccurate? Largely because of mental uncertainty. Take your simplest piece and play it at a normal tempo. Keep your mind upon it, and inaccuracy disappears. However, take a more ambitious piece, play it just a little faster than you are properly able to do, and inaccuracy immediately appears. That is the whole secret. There is no other.

It takes strength of will to play slowly. It is easy enough to let ambitions to play rapidly carry one away. I remember a student who would play the Chopin *A-Minor Chromatic Etude* (Example V–1) at a perfectly teriffic rate of speed.

Ex. V-1   Chopin Etude, Op. 10, No. 2

At the end both the performer and the auditor were breathless in the apprehension of mistakes, among which there were bound to be several blurs, smears and other faults. It gave no artistic pleasure because there was no repose, no poise. Only by hard work was this pupil made to see that she should practice very slowly, then just a little faster and finally never at a speed that would lead to mental and digital confusion. There is no limit to speed, if you can play accurately.

One good test of accuracy is to find out whether you can play a rapid composition at any speed. It is often more difficult to play a piece at an intermediate than at a very rapid speed. The metronome is an excellent check upon speed. Start playing with it very slowly, and gradually advance the speed with succeeding repetitions. Then try to do the same thing without the metronome. The student must develop a sense of tempos. In fact, the whole literature of music is characterized by different tempos. The pupil should learn to feel almost instinctively how fast the various movements in the Beethoven Sonatas should be, how fast the Chopin Nocturnes or the Schumann *Nachstücke* should be. Of course there always will be a margin of difference in the tempos of different individuals; but exaggerated tempos—either too fast or too slow—are among the most common forms of inaccuracy.

Two Important Factors

Before leaving the matter of accuracy, it may be said that two other factors play an important part. The fingering must be the best possible for the given passage; it must be adhered to in every successive performance; and the hand position (or shall we say "hand slant") must be the best adaptable to the passage. The easiest position is always the best. Often pupils struggle with difficult passages and declare them impossible, when a mere change of the hand position, such as raising or lowering the wrist or slanting the hand laterally, would solve the problem. It is impossible to give the student any universal panacea to fit different passages, but a good rule is to experiment and find what is easiest for the individual hand. Rubinstein, who so often struck wrong notes in his later years when his uncontrollable artistic vehemence often carried him beyond himself, was terribly insistent upon accuracy with his pupils. He never forgave wrong note slips, or mussy playing.

One of the chief offenders in the matter of inaccuracy is the left hand. Scores of students play with unusual certainty with the right hand who seem to think nothing of making blunders with the left hand. If they only knew how important this matter is! The left hand gives quality and character to playing. In all passages except where it is introduced as a simple accompaniment, its role is equally important with that of the right hand. An operatic performance with the great Galli-Curci as the soprano and, let us say, Caruso as the tenor, would be execrable if the contralto and the bass made the audience miserable by their poor quality and their inaccuracy. Practice your left hand as though you had no right hand and had to get everything from the left hand. Play your left hand parts over and over, giving them individuality, independence and character, and your playing will improve one hundred per cent.

If you are suspicious about your left hand, and you doubtless have good reason to be, why not imagine that your right hand is "out of commission" for two or three days and devote your entire attention to your left hand? You will probably note a great difference in the character of your playing when you put them together. Left hand pieces and left hand studies are useful, but they are oddities, "freaks."

Some Things About Staccato

Staccato, considered as touch, is often marred by surface noises of the fingers tapping on the keys. Perhaps you have never noticed this. In some passages this percussive noise seems to contribute to the effect but in general it must be used with caution. A very simple expedient reduces this noise and increases the lightness and character of the staccato. It is merely the raising of the wrist. By raising the wrist, the stroke comes from a different angle, is lighter, but nonetheless secure and makes for ease in very fleet passages.

Try the measures in Example V–2 from Rubinstein's *Staccato Etude,* with your wrist in normal position. Then raise the wrist and note the lightness you have contributed to your playing.

Ex. V‑2 Staccato Etude
Allegro vivace M.M. ♩ = 63–72

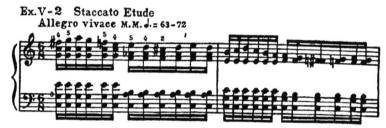

Finger staccatos, produced by wiping the keys, are also effective when properly applied. There is also, of course, a kind of brilliant staccato such as one finds in the Chopin Opus 32, No. 2 (Example V–3), and in other passages, where the action of the whole forearm is involved. In this the wrist is held stiff. But in every and all cases let the fingers look down—see and feel the keys and not look at the ceiling!

Ex. V‑3 Chopin Nocturnes, Op. 32, No. 2

THE BASIS OF BEAUTIFUL LEGATO

The word legato, meaning bound, has misled thousands of students. It is easy to bind notes—but "How?"—that is the question. There is always a moment when there are two sounds. If one sound is continued too long after a succeeding one is played, the legato is bad. On the other hand, if it is not continued enough the effect is likely to be portamento rather than legato (always remembering that the word portamento as used in piano playing has an almost entirely different meaning from the use of the same word in singing).

Well-played legato notes on the piano must float into each other. Now here is the point. The floating effect is not possible unless the quality of the tone of the notes is similar. In other words all the notes must be of the same tonal color. A variation in the kind of touch employed and a legato phrase may be ruined. The notes in a legato phrase may be likened to strings of beads. In the playing of many pupils the strings of tonal beads are of all different colors, sizes, shapes and qualities in one single phrase. The touch control varies in the different notes so greatly that such a simple phrase as the following from Schumann's *Träumerei* might be likened to Example V–4.

Ex. V-4   Schumann's Träumerei

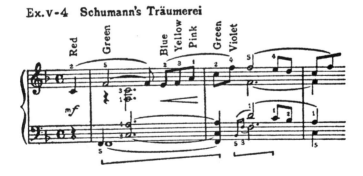

Surely the effect will be heightened by maintaining the same touch for at least one phrase.

When the colors are blended as in the prism, instead of being mixed up by ill-selected contrasts, the effect is far more beautiful, judged by artistic and aesthetic standards. Play *Träumerei* a few times, preserving the character of the phrases by careful observance of what you have learned in the previous chapters regarding the principles of beautiful tone production at the keyboard.

Another excellent work in which to make a study of legato is the *F Minor Nocturne* of Chopin (Example V–5).

Ex. V-5   Chopin Nocturne, Op. 55, No. 1

One more principle in the matter of legato playing, before we dismiss it in this all too short discussion of a subject which might easily take many pages. The greater the length of the notes in a given passage in a pianoforte composition, the more difficult the legato. Have you ever realized that? Note that we have mentioned the piano particularly. On the violin the situation is quite different. Take Bach's *Air on the G String* with its long drawn out notes. They could have been made twice as long if necessary; but this would be impossible upon the piano, because this instrument's sound starts to diminish the moment it is struck. Therefore, in a legato in very slow passages, the student confronts a real problem. He must sound the note with sufficient ringing tone so that it will not disappear before the next note; and in striking the succeeding note he must take into account the amount of diminution so that the new note will not be introduced with a "bump."

Scales afford an excellent means for the study of both legato and staccato. Scales are valueless unless the student practices them with his "ears" as well as his fingers. Mozart was accused of playing a note in a composition (which required both hands at the extremities of the piano) with his nose. If students could learn to practice with their ears open and keen to hear niceties of tone, the task of the teacher would be a far more enjoyable and profitable one and music throughout the world would advance very materially.

All that has been said in this chapter of these conferences has an important bearing upon the succeeding chapter, which has to do with Rhythm, Velocity, Bravura Playing and Pedal Study. Accuracy, beautiful legato and refined staccato are so important, however, that every student who gives these matters extra attention will surely be immensely rewarded. In fact it would be a very good plan to take a book of standard studies or pieces very much below your grade of accomplishment and by means of careful, thoughtful, devout study, in which your "ears" play an equal role with your fingers, take phrase after phrase and play them over and over again.

A beautiful touch, a beautiful legato, will not come by merely wishing for it. It will not come by hours of inattentive playing at the keyboard. It is very largely a matter of developing your tonal sense, your aesthetic ideals, and mixing them with your hours of practice. Try practicing for beauty as well as practicing for technic. Technic is worthless in your playing, if it means nothing more to you than making machines of your hands. I am confident that centuries of practice are wasted throughout the world because the element of beauty is cast aside. Thousands of pianoforte recitals are given in the great music centers of the world by aspiring students every year. They look forward to great careers. They play their Liszt Rhapsodies, their Concertos and their Sonatas, often with most commendable accuracy, but with very little of the one great quality which the world wants and for which it holds its highest rewards—Beauty.

If this series of conferences succeeds in turning the attention of a few hundred students towards the need for beauty, and the means for expressing it in every moment of pianoforte practice, I shall feel repaid for giving the time to them.

STOP AND LISTEN

Do you express the *composer's* thought and mood?
Do you express what *you* feel and wish?
Whatever it is, by all means express something!

CHAPTER VI

People Who Memorize Readily

In the final discussion of this series it may seem wise here and there to recapitulate some of the principles already enunciated. Let us discuss, however, for a few moments, by way of an interlude, the all-important matter of memorizing music. The custom of playing everything by memory is of comparatively recent introduction. Very few musicians at the time of Mozart, Haydn or Beethoven ever thought it necessary. Just as at the present time it has come to be the custom of certain orchestral conductors to dispense with the score, it gradually became the thing to appear in concert without the printed notes and very few artists of any considerable standing have played with notes to any extent during the last twenty-five years. I am told that Pugno, the French pianist, did employ them in America.

There can be no question that the act of turning pages in full view of two or three thousand people may well disturb the atmosphere of the concert room. It is therefore considered indispensable to memorize. This does not mean, however, that one should essay to memorize the entire musical literature as some students elect to do. Learn those things that are necessary, that will be useful. Do not tax the memory.

Do not place too much stress upon those who memorize readily. Some people seem to be gifted with a kind of mental glibness. They make their mental photographs with a kind of cinematographic rapidity; and the impress is likely to disappear quite as rapidly. If you find that you memorize slowly, do not let it bother you. I have found that the students who depend too much upon their natural gifts in memorizing make many mistakes. Their memories are neither reliable or accurate. When they need the memory most it fails them. I say this purposely because I know that a great many students have a terrible struggle in the matter of memorizing. Stick to it. The more effort you put in your memorizing the firmer will be the impression upon your brain negative.

Memorize phrase by phrase, not measure by measure. The phrase is the musical unit, not the measure, unless the phrase lengths happen to conform to the measure lengths. The thing to remember is the thought, not the symbols. When you remember a poem you do not remember the alphabetical symbols, but the poet's beautiful vision, his thought pictures. So many students waste hours of time trying to remember black notes. Absurd! They mean nothing. Get the thought, the composer's idea; that is the thing that sticks.

For the same reason that one should memorize by phrases, one should also have a firm grasp of the elements of harmony to memorize well. Chords are musical words. The arrangement of chords is not as arbitrary as the arrangement of words in a sentence, but the sequence of chords in harmony is an immense help to the memory.

In my own case my memory seemed to be asleep until I was twelve years old. Then I memorized only with the greatest difficulty. Now, by dint of great experience, I memorize very easily. It is all a matter of persistence, time and training. It is for such a reason that I would encourage all those who are now having a struggle with memorizing. What you do memorize,

memorize well. There are amateurs who seem to be able to play the greater part of the whole literature of the piano from memory, but who do not play any one piece really finely. Of course, the concert pianist has stored away in his subconscious mind literally millions of notes. He makes up his programs for a season—if he is called upon to play a certain concerto he has not played for some time, he practices upon it and it comes back to him with a readiness dependent upon the thoroughness with which he originally learned it.

THE DAILY PRACTICE

Daily drill in memorizing, if only just a little, is better than studying memorizing now and then. It is the regular practice that counts.

Four hours a day of practice is good measure. Over-practicing is just as bad as under-practicing. It should be the younger student's aim and desire to get done with technic as soon as possible. There is no short cut. One cannot go around or under the mountain. One must climb straight over it. Therefore in the earlier lessons more attention must be given to technic than in the later lessons when a really masterly technic has been developed. The trouble is that most students seem to look upon it the other way. Two hours a day for those who are not advanced in music (not beginners by any means) are not too much for technic. I do not see how one can climb over the great mountain of modern technic at a less speed than two hours a day. Otherwise, they would be old men and women before they could hope to compare with others in these days of enormous technical competition. Everybody knows that technic is only a means to an end; but without this means one does not reach the end. There may not be anything very beautiful about the great, grimy engine of an automobile; but if one would get to the journey's end—to the dreamland of wonderful trees, gorgeous flowers and entrancing beauty—he must have the means. You must travel just so many scale miles and arpeggio miles and octave miles before you arrive at the musical dreamland of interesting execution and interpretation.

Always divide your practice periods. Do your technic at one time and your pieces at another. Approach the two sections with different aspects.

Avoid worry and distractions of any kind when you are practicing. Your mind must be every minute on what you are doing, or the value of your practice is lessened enormously. By intense concentration, love of your work and the spirit in which you approach it, you can do more in a half hour than in an hour spent purposelessly. Do not think you have been practicing, if you have played a single note with your mind on anything else.

When you practice in the right spirit you don't know what it is to get tired. I often practice three or four hours and hardly realize that I have been practicing at all.

Secure Variety in Practice

Variety in practice is most important. Repeating monotonously over and over again in treadmill fashion is the very worst kind of practice. It is both stupid and unnecessary. Take the scale of C. It may be played in hundreds of ways, with different rhythms, with different speeds and with different touches. The hands may be varied. One hand may play legato and the other staccato. Practice in this way, using your brains and your ingenuity, and your practice will not be a bore to you.

Practice in rhythm is something which American students in particular should not fail to secure. The student should look upon the rhythm of a piece as part of the personality of the piece. It should be marked by a strong vigorous design in the background. The Bohemians, Hungarians, Poles and the Russians seem to have an instinctive sense of rhythm. The Americans seem to fail in it. It puts me to my wits' ends to know how to develop this sense of rhythm, which is one of the most human things in music. Playing duets helps to develop it; and of course hearing a great deal of strong rhythmic music is an aid. This can be heard in concerts and also by means of the talking machine.

Accompanying an instrumentalist or a singer with a strong rhythmic sense is also a very good way of awakening the lethargic pupil to his rhythmic shortcomings. It is sometimes something of a shock to the young pianist to be asked to accompany such a singer for the first time. They find themselves being dragged along into new thought channels of which they have known but little.

Rhythm should not be thought of as something dead. It is live, vital, elastic. Of course, in the deadly thump, thump of the military march of the Schubert type, there is not the sprightly rhythm that one finds in a Chopin Etude. Whether the piece is played slower or faster the rhythmic design must not be obscured. It must always be there.

ACQUIRING VELOCITY

First of all, let me admit that there does seem to be a physical limitation in the matter of velocity, and this differs in different people. It is mental as well as muscular and nervous. Certain pupils do have limitations. The ability to acquire abnormal velocity by no means insures musical ability. Some pupils can play "like lightning," but can hardly do anything else well. Do not overrate velocity. Some develop it very quickly, and some acquire it only after great patience and persistence. Therefore, there is no hard and fast rule upon how to develop it. Perhaps the best general principle is the acquisition of the habit of playing with an extremely loose, floating hand. Rigidity of muscles and velocity never go together. Personally, I was always able to play with great rapidity. One of the serious mistakes that Safonoff made with me was that when he found that I could do a thing unusually well he would indulge me in it. He never gave me enough of the works in which there was no occasion for bravura, virtuosity and velocity. Develop your weak points; the strong points will take care of themselves.

The Danger of Bravura

There is something about all of us that fascinates us with anything that is showy. When we have a piece that "goes off" like a lot of fireworks, it intrigues us. Such pieces are dangerous; they lead one away from the finer side of one's art.

In bravura playing, the spirit and character of the piece is everything. Bravura playing is daring. One elects to play a brilliant passage, takes a chance, and accomplishes it. One is thrilled with success and then proceeds to waste valuable time in developing it to the disadvantage of other phases of technic.

Bravura playing is also attempted all too early by students. They want to play the Tchaikowsky Concerto before they can properly play a Czerny exercise. I once found one student who didn't know anything but bravura pieces. He was able to astonish all his relatives, but could not dream of giving a well-balanced program before a musical audience.

Another danger of bravura is that many seem to look upon it as a kind of musical scrimmage. As the tempo and the dynamic force are increased in a brilliant passage, the notes become more obscured and confused, the octaves are mixed up and the trills mussy. Good bravura playing is just the opposite, and as the effect begins to "soar and resound" there should be more and more clarity.

The Danger of the Pedal

If there is a danger in bravura, there is also a danger in pedaling. So much latitude can be taken in pedaling (and, indeed, who would make hard and fast rules for pedaling?) that the novice uses the pedal like a kalsomine brush with which he might paint the back fence. The pedal demands study, meticulous study. It should be used with the same intelligence and definiteness as the fingers. It should be applied in the fraction of a second and released at just the right moment.

One of the dangers is in not releasing the pedal at the right time. When to raise the foot is just as important as when to put it down. The best pedal effects in artistic playing are those in which the audience does not realize that there is a pedal at all.

Regular pedaling (that is, when the pedal is depressed when the note is struck) and syncopated pedaling (depressing the pedal after the note has been struck) both have their uses. When playing a series of chords, use the syncopated pedaling, for in no other way can the sound be made continuous. It saves the piano from sounding like a xylophone.

Pedaling is all in the knowing how. I employ a full pedal, a half pedal and a one-quarter pedal or just a touch. In some of these effects the pedal just barely removes the dampers from the wires; sometimes they touch slightly, producing a delightful harp-like effect. (This effect is rarely heard upon an upright piano as the mechanism is different.)

One of the dangers of pedaling is in the so-called atmospheric effects. One knows that in a beautiful Corot painting the sharp outlines are almost nowhere to be seen. Corot, the master, lost them in a wonderful atmosphere. Thus, in certain modern works of music these outlines may be softened by the very skillful use of the pedal. There is no hard and fast rule, each phrase is a law unto itself.

The pedaling in a Haydn Sonata and the pedaling in a Chopin Berceuse are as different as the brush technic that one would find in a Pre-Raphaelite painting and in a Millet. They represent different epochs and must be treated differently.

What is so fascinating as the art of music; and how can it be approached with more charm by the individual than through the pianoforte? There is hardly anything so hideous as bad piano playing, and scarcely anything more beautiful than the masterly interpretation of a great composition by a great artist. Surely, it is worth all the study and far more, to acquire an intimacy with this wonderful instrument which brings so many of the gorgeous treasures of the tone world so near to the individual.